DADDY

Also by Michael Montlack

Cool Limbo (NYQ Books)

My Diva (University of Wisconsin Press)

Daddy

Michael Montlack

The New York Quarterly Foundation, Inc.
Beacon, New York

NYQ Books™ is an imprint of The New York Quarterly Foundation, Inc.

The New York Quarterly Foundation, Inc.
P. O. Box 470
Beacon, NY 12508

www.nyq.org

First Edition

Set in New Baskerville

Title Set in Stud-Regular

Layout and Design by Raymond P. Hammond

Cover Illustration: *Seahorse,* 9" x 12" charcoal and watercolor pencil on toned paper by Christopher Shields

Back Cover Illustration: *Daddy Seahorse* by Marc Brudzinski

Author Photo by Dorianne Laux

Library of Congress Control Number: 2020931915

ISBN: 978-1-63045-059-5

Daddy

Acknowledgments

American Journal of Poetry: "Schroeder" & "Unceremonial"
Assaracus: "A High Way to Hell"
   "Dickorum (Grindr)"
Barrow Street: "Purple Haze"
   "Sonnet for the Dowager Countess"
Bellevue Literary Review: "Toast"
Border Crossing: "Masculinity" & "Parade"
The Cimarron Review: "My Niece Kimberly"
The Cincinnati Review: *"Ancient Aliens"*
The Cossack Review: "From Poland with Love"
Duende: "Do Our Parents Ever Really Die?"
The Gay & Lesbian Review: "Cherry Grove Carla"
Gertrude: "End Game"
Gingerbread House: "Stevie"
Good Men Project: "Dickorum (Nonchalance)"
Gulf Stream: "Dickorum (Heterosexuals)"
Los Angeles Review: "Ruth"
Locus Point: "In Her Voice"
Luna Luna Magazine: "My Sister Michele Never Read the Book"
Magma Poetry: "Rock River, Vermont"
Mudfish: "And then there was fire…"
Narrative Northeast: "Esmeralda"
   "Haiku Triptych: Portland"
   "In Tamika's Basement"
The Nervous Breakdown: "Daddy"
The Offing: "One Sparrow"
The Ocean State Review: "Finding My Biological Parents"
Peculiar: "Board Meeting" & "Loft"
Poet Lore: "My Father's Workshop"
Tupelo Quarterly: "The Passion of Sergius and Bacchus"

Bearing the Mask (anthology):   "Granddaddy Jess"
Stonewall Legacy (anthology):   "Daddy: A Delicate Diatribe"
   "Homosexuality"

for my parents

Howie & Claire

Contents

Mother

Father

Daddy

How to Mother Like a Man

I like how the male seahorse gives
birth, making it easier for the female
exhausted from egg production,
how the round, puffed belly looks
like my father's beer gut, how
despite the protrusion, he appears
sleek, in suspension, ornately
ridged, that curlicue tail coiled
demurely until it's ready to link
with his mate, who inflates him
with life, a live chess board piece
moving nonchalantly in the current,
gentle but with intention, a knight
really, doing whatever it takes
to protect the Queen.

after Ada Limón's "How to Triumph Like a Girl"

Daddy

"I saw you, Walt Whitman, childless, lonely old grubber, poking among the meats in the refrigerator and eyeing the grocery boys."

—*Allen Ginsberg*

Daddy: Mythologies

You should've seen his face
when I said I'd never had sex
without condoms. Was it pity?
Disappointment? Or fascination.

As if I were a unicorn. On display.
In my bed. His palm petting
my chest. As if to calm a beast.
Or soothe a timid child.

In his mid-thirties, a little more
than a decade younger than me,
wasn't AIDS a ghost story for him?

Was it part of my job to narrate
that epic? To conjure the 90s
Castro, where I came out,
where I nearly passed out,
my first Friday night at the bars,
seeing men in their mid-thirties,
a little older than me, so emaciated,
so drawn, I had flashbacks
to Hebrew School imagery
of Holocaust survivors.

Only these men would not
survive. I tried not to imagine
my own face back then: Pity?
Fear? Shock? As if they were
unicorns. About to disappear.

I didn't want to disappear,
I tell him. But I can't explain
how abandoning condoms

feels like abandoning those men.
Even when he reminds me
about the wonders of Prep,
the intimacy I'm missing,
the fear I am clinging to.

I want to explain that fear,
for me, is like homage now.

Instead I tell him we can't date,
blaming our age difference.
Really I don't want to explain
how I've only been monogamous,
knowing he prefers throuples.

Too many unicorns.
Why add a dinosaur.

Benjamin Un-Button-ed

How ancient I was
as a child. Contained
like a nesting doll—
little old man at its core.
The worrywart warning
my twin sister to stop
jumping on the bed.
You'll break a spring!

Now nearing fifty
I beg my best buddy
to rent a bouncy house
for his summer bash:
We'll oil the sucker up.
Load it with naked gay guys.
Bears! Come on!

Yeah, the once scrawny
sissy boy, so heavy
with secrecy, fear
of being seen, obsessively
monitoring where
his eyes might creep.

Now daring neighbors
to *Jump on in! Join us!*
Unless they would rather
lounge in their yards
and *Look all you like!*

Dickorum

                            was adopting
that world-weary nonchalance—
shedding the awe you might've felt
about anything out of the ordinary
or downright lewd: Like that manic
spandex-clad drag queen whose tuck
came undone during her first number,
blowjobs in the john (stall door open),
or the colorful butt plug collection
arcing like a rainbow over the juke—
Debbie Harry or Sandra Bernhard
lounging on a sofa across from yours.
It should all appear whateverly. Not
worth mentioning. In fact, *you* should
appear whateverly. Like you wonder why
you even appeared here in the first place.
As if you will disappear, as soon as
the drag queen finishes her set.

The Passion of Sergius and Bacchus

Chained and dressed in women's clothes
before Army officials dragged you down
dusty village roads—hardly a 4th Century
Pride parade—for sustaining your selves,
and your vows, closet Christians refusing
to bow. Spectators expecting Jupiter's
thunderbolt to strike the temple floor—

Bacchus, forgive us if we try to forget
the torture you endured, wondering instead
if you were named after the jolly winemaker
with a hard-on for Adonis. Retelling ourselves
that tender part of the legend when your spirit
consoles Sergius with a promise to reunite.
(Only after they'd come to take his head.)
But rest assured, boys. You remain adored,
your brave love iconic, well preserved.

Scholars be damned! Let them say
what they will. We've already married you—
to each other and ourselves—seeing far
beyond the fury to your furry calves
and battered ankles glistening in the sun
below those muddied, tattered hems.

A High Way to Hell

Truck stop: public turnstile club
for spies of the tight smiles,
a homesick sucker's release circuit.
Shaken bottles of mood mounting:
white rush into the porcelain flush.
A remembering of animals, cuts, throats,
awkward belongings, somehow comfortable
fever. Yesterday's crumpled route
to recovered indulgence? *Don't spit!*
Your devotionless devotion. Denim-ed
undoings. And then, *Please, Sir. Some more?*
When too many was not enough. *Get!*
A grip on a hairy ankle: a sailor boy's anchor.
Fluid expressway: snake of yellow lights.
Boy, where do ya think you're going?
Slithering toward exhaustion. Watch now.
Yeah, watch. See how often it never comes.

after Chip Livingston's "The Favorable Witness"

Loft

When the fire escape icicles promised
        something stripped and craggy,
something beyond salvation,
        something immune to prayer,
the orange blossoms in his voice
        released like rain each time
he called me into the studio
        to offer my uncurated opinion
of a brushstroke or shadow,
        the limestone floor chilling
my soles through the woolen socks
        his mother gave me for Christmas,
his pupils gray-black and charged
        as flint, a stare daring me
to be honest, another version of myself
        lured by his baritone, a siren
so mesmerizing I would forget
        how beneath his layered oils
and lingering linseed scent
        lay a frigid white sheet of gesso.

Schroeder

Wasn't I like a wife in the wings willing
to stab her own eyeballs with toothpicks
then serve them as hors d'oeuvres
at another one of his opening nights?
Yes, like Lucy sprawled (sometimes
spreadeagled!) across his piano, begging
him to take a request—to include me
somewhere in the repertoire—to just
look up through his blonde bangs
and wink at my favorite part. But he
could only see through the porthole
of music, even when I jumped from
the plane I hired to skywrite his name,
those parachute chords catching my pits
so I'd descend with arms outstretched,
as if expecting a hug.

If Only We Met in an Emergency

I'd be more certain.

Nothing catastrophic.
A mere brush with death
would do, a storm at sea
so I might watch your knuckles
whiten as you undo the knots,
trying to release our lifeboat.

It doesn't seem enough—
how well you treat servers,
how generous the tip.
Let's see you man that boat,
how fast you can row.

Forget sweet voicemails
on lunch breaks. I'd rather
listen to your B-side, lyrics
you scrawled in a dungeon,
bleary-eyed, urine-soaked,
begging for sunlight, water,
a last chance to write home.

That chicken scratch—more you
than any Hallmark or wedding vow.

I'm not wishing any harm
but a broken window gives way
to the cold and stench
along with the pretty view.

Sue me if I favor a minor fiasco
to suggest how sturdy a skeleton,
a rigmarole vigorous enough

to shake free the most stubborn fruit
so I can suck truth from its pit.

Near-naked selfies on the beach
reveal so little. I want to know
what kind of man will emerge
when a child disappears in the waves.
Show me your sweaty close-up
from the climax of our biopic.

Maybe that'll put the kibosh
on all the stupid questions,
allowing a clear glimpse
of myself, that panicked child
flailing his arms in a current
unknowable and urgent as love.

Haiku Triptych: Portland

First Date

scruffy tattooed men
straddle bikes to kiss in rain
fair trade coffee breath

Valentine

your vintage plaid shirt
frayed like the one my ex wore
recycles my heart

Breakup

your chickens are gone
so is your recipe box
but the food cart's mine

Ancient Aliens

While you're *Just doin' weekend chores*
with your boyfriend (or is it fiancé now?),
I'm gorging again on The History Channel,
trying to convince myself I might meet
someone at the gym if only I could levitate
from my sofa with the same ease and grace
Chinese Myths assigned to "flying dragons"
some Ph.D. (with A Flock of Seagulls haircut)
insists were aircraft awing naïve ancestors.

They just didn't have a name for it.

I didn't have a name for it either. The alien
sensation that descended that afternoon
your boyfriend—my long-time friend—
finally introduced his *new beau*. A handshake
charged like the jolt that same Ph.D.
suggests was not the lightning of Zeus
scalding humans from Mount Olympus
(perhaps for a vice like coveting?) but
a glowing beam, some otherworldly force
from some bird-thing landing from beyond.
The aliens suddenly all the men I believed
I had loved. Dwarfed now from the top
of a pyramid I couldn't recall climbing.
Always falling short. Not enough. Not *it*.

Whatever *it* was.

I just never had a name for it. Until you
offered yours. And I was struck dumb,
a stargazing primitive willing to carve
your likeness into cavern walls, learn
your language, spend a whole lifetime
flattening the earth into a landing pad
in case you might visit again.

Rock River, Vermont
(Bet Frost Never Stopped by *These* Woods)

What do the locals say when they see
the line of cars snaking along the side
of the highway, an unofficial parade
of gay guys bee-lining for the woods,
totes stuffed with chips, thermos-ed
cocktails, sunscreen and lube?
How do parents explain when kids
in backseats ask, *Where they all going?*
Maybe Vermonters appreciate the summer
business boost. Maybe some relish a little
raunch to salt their quaint, quiet state.

Either way, there's no hunting these bears.
(The land purchased by and for gay men.)
If only our gym teachers could see us now.
Breathy middle-agers scaling muddy cliffs
high above the river. Dauntless. Determined.
A thirty-minute hike to the watering hole
dotted with one-or-two hundred naked men,
chit-chatting or napping after a foray up the hill,
tiered like a wedding cake, for an afternoon
circle jerk under a canopy of maple leaves,
toes wriggling in the soil, like happy worms.

Dickorum

        is your boss messaging you—
after seeing your Grindr profile one night—
to ask if the monthly budget analysis is done…
before he compliments your cockshot.
(In a parenthesized PS.)

Dickorum is answering: "Sorry, I'll need
another day or two on that. And thanks! I like
your fisting pics. Your hubby's talented."

It's also immediately realizing (after hitting send)
that maybe that isn't his hubby (Oh god, it's Bob
from Accounting!) but not correcting yourself,
just letting it go.

Finally, Dickorum is not even blushing as you
pass his cubicle the next day. No wink from him.
No smile. Nada. Just a "How'd you make out?"
that you almost answer before realizing he doesn't
mean the budget figures. It was a loaded greeting,
gay Morse code. So just keep walking. And sure—
take an extended gander at Bob in Accounting
if you want, but not long enough to suggest
you're interested. Unless you're into fisting.

Because Dickorum says don't cock tease.
Or ass tease. Or put up your "dukes"…
unless you mean it. Because Dickorum
forgives raunchiness. Not false advertising
(like your boss's age on Grindr).

"I'm 84," Terrence said.

"I should be demented." He chuckled,
slipping the miniature Jameson bottle
under the table. "Would you kindly—
the cap's quite stubborn." His partner
Gary fanned out a menu wide enough
for me to use as cover. "We do love
this place," Terrence whispered. "But
the bartender can be...well, stingy."

Gary shifted the menu so I could fill
the tumbler discreetly. "What,"
Terrence said. "I swim every day.
Take NYU classes to keep sharp.
And yes—enjoy a regular nightcap."

We toasted. "To Kiss!" A 6-year-old Tabby
they rescued that week. "A true survivor,"
Gary said. "From a hurricane down south."

"We wanted an older cat," Terrence added.
I remembered our previous dinner. How
Gary struggled to get a server's attention.
"Age makes you invisible," he said.
More observation than complaint.

I always ached when they thanked me
for checking in. "We're friends," I'd scold.
Recalling the day Terrence proposed
occasional coffees with Gary. Instead of
my weekly sessions. "I'm always here,"
he said. "But our work seems done."
My friends thought it crazy. "Is that even

professional? To hang with your therapist?"
"He's not my therapist now. They're like
uncles—the coolest uncles ever."

"Remember Emma?" Terrence asked.
A Persian they had when I began seeing him.
"How I loved her." His eyes glistening
the way they did the night he explained
how he was thrust into the AIDS crisis.
"Before it had a name." How his protégé,
a gay grad student, was one of the first to go.

"I trained for family court. But suddenly
I was helping young men to die." Terrence
on his sofa, a generous Jameson on his knee,
pausing before naming that student. Steve.
Repeating it. Repeating it. As if to conjure him.
So I might see for myself. "How kind he was."

Gary said what Terrence was too modest to say.
"He went to the hospital every day. To visit."

The ice clinked as Terrence took a swig.
"When he was gone, I came home one night
to a check in the mail. For my time!" he cried.
"For helping him die!" Emma leaped onto
his lap, to comfort him. "Can you imagine?
He wanted to pay me. Pay! But I was his friend.
I loved him. He owed me nothing. Nothing.
Not even a thanks."

Homosexuality

So long at the bottom of the well—
occasional shafts of sunlight
disturbing the darkness—my eyes
calibrated to decipher shadows
for other nocturnal creatures.

Always there were none.

When the rope finally lowered,
I was so delirious with fever
I nearly looped my neck with it,
instead of my waist, expecting
to be booby-trapped at the top.

It's okay. I'll get you outta there!
The voice familiar—my own?
Maybe. I'd never really heard
what I sounded like. Unless this
was the trap? Wait! Too late—

he was pulling me through
the well's mouth. Gathering me
into his arms. *Breathe. Breathe.*
Everything seemed jeweled
with a glare. Even his badge.

Engraved with my name?

Preoccupied by the charge
I inherited, I almost forgot
my note scratched nightly
into the well's stone walls:

By the time you read this…
Scars in my fingerprints.

Daddy: A Delicate Diatribe

Crawl a little closer—you might detect a whiff
of lavender oil in my whip's handle, or maybe, if lucky,
some stubborn glitter to lick from my boot sole.

Don't make me tell you again. *DUNGEON RULES*
on the cinderblock walls: a rainbow of pastel chalks,
the barback's penmanship elegant as Grandmama's.

And don't be afraid—let your power slide
like a bra strap, so demure, over that furry shoulder.
Just don't make me tell you again. Whimper—

I'll hear only manliness. Cling like a barnacle
to my calf—I'll gauge your strength. Press
the right button, pig, and I might weep with you.

Tugging you closer. Closer. So you can inhale
the musk of my hairy nipple, allowing me
to serve while you nurse.

Purple Haze

how *groovy*, bean-bagging
    in my big sister's room
painted green like her pot plants
    our mother watered daily,
groaning *Your poor baby ferns!*
    Why are they so droopy?—
my sister (eyes never lifting
    from her *Creem* magazine)
smirked as I squirmed
    below Jimi, Mick and Rod
postering the walls—bare-
    chested, long-haired, hip-
hugged—thrusting mics
    at wet lips snarled
in silent wails daring me to *Come*
    back! when no one was home
so we bad boys could finally
    rock and roll alone.

Strange Big Fish

Like birds of paradise, we pecked
appetizers at an Amazonian place
Felipe said everyone was raving about.

A rooftop dinner for Natasha, a dancer
from Uruguay, in Rio for her birthday.
So at home here with friends. At home
in her body. At home even with me,
the *Gringo,* five minutes into meeting.

Pablo palming my lap as he translated
dishes. Mostly strange big fish. Natasha
suggesting wines, fluent in Portuguese.
I hadn't studied a word. Afraid to dig in
too deep. In a place too far away. Pablo—
seven years younger, seven inches shorter—
liked rescuing his big helpless baby:
What can we feed you tonight, Daddy?

Usually lost in the music of their words,
I gathered only names and cities: familiar
flowers that floated on a Portuguese river
too rapid to swim. Felipe insisting we stay:
Para la samba!

But we'd leave for Fortaleza. The calmer
Carnival. *Baby steps for Pablo's baby!*
Natasha winked. *A New Yorker who hates
crowds?* I confessed I only came for Pablo.

Of course, she said. Her accent soft like her
shoulder's curve, a sigh in the pre-Carnival
quiet almost as charged as Pablo's fingertips
combing the hair on my thigh, her eyes
trembling candles in the dark. *But won't you
suffer?* she asked. *When the trip is over?*

Neither of us answering. In either language.

Daddy

They say it unabashedly.

Sometimes a twenty-something,
half my size, will lean across the bar
to touch my leg. *Hey, Daddy,*
he says, *can I buy you a beer?*

Others in their late thirties
or mid-forties, some even
older than me. And still they
say it. In hushed baby talk.
Or a taunting whisper.
Part plea, part demand.
A bratty whine. Usually
punctuated with a hungry sigh
when I take off my belt.

They don't want discipline.
Or humiliation. Just someone
bigger, I think. Someone hairier.
Someone who might demonstrate
self-assurance—easily mistaken
for power in the dark
after a couple drinks.

Daddy, don't, they groan,
aiming their asses at me,
like cannons, thighs already
ajar. *Please, Daddy, don't!*

My hard-on keeps me from
giggling. And wondering
how I got here. How they—
in their own self-assurance—
have cast me as their lead,
though clearly at best
I'm a supporting actor.

Board Meeting

So much can unhinge on a hump-day daydream.
Today: a sailor on leave with gams like scissors.
Yeah, serve me up a slice of *his* pumpkin bread—
To go! I'll just keep him in my back pocket.
For a coffee-break lift. My little swirl of milk.
Watch him twirl in my fingers like a paper parasol.
I can crown him. Or cripple him. I kid you not.
His résumé bullets: *Special Skills.* An executive decision
as I draw the office blinds. Call me a corporate heretic.
Another in-box indiscretion. I can almost see them:
Colleagues congesting the board room. Suits
and ties. All prepared for my latest PowerPoint
while I carefully tie up my un-suited sailor, offering him
a mandatory seminar in customer service.

Dickorum

is being the sponge
for all those graphic things
heterosexuals suddenly confess
upon finding out you're gay—
mostly sexual stuff (wanting
a same-sex experience, a ménage
without their partner, sex toys
made out of office supplies
or Sesame Street hand puppets):
fantasies they'd never share
with their straight friends.

Dickorum is feigning shock
at the details, saying, *Oh, no,
you didn't!* in all the right places.
And urging them to be brave
enough to express themselves.

Face it: Dickorum is accepting
the responsibility of helping others
attain your sexual sophistication
and openness. Even if you're just
a mama's boy at heart.

Mother

"...*now the unison suddenly breaks; I have to go on by myself, no maestro, no score to follow.*"

—*C.K. Williams*

Toast

Once a woman who lost her mother
told me the story of a guru rushing
to satisfy his dying mentor's last wish.

For bread. "You see," the woman said,
"if he died with an unfulfilled desire,
big or small, he'd risk reincarnation."

She believed her mother's dementia—
an almost-infancy—had completed
such a cycle. Her mother, never truly
nurtured, finally cared for like a baby.

*

                Later, my sister shared
my mother's last words: *Get Michael!*

I didn't make it in time.

For months I've dreamed of a curtain.
No window. Just the curtain. Hanging
in the center of an empty room. Heavy
velvet. Dark grey. Swaying in a breeze
I can see but not feel.

I think my reincarnation's inevitable.

At night I whisper: *Shall we be friends
next time? Cousins? How about sisters?*

Though I am certain: I will be her mother.

"Don't listen to her. Listen through her."

—Stevie Nicks

Who can trust words anyway—
man-made gadgets, subject
to the rack of interpretation,
so flexible they're flimsy
or so rigid they snap.

It's all tone in the end.
A growl is a growl is a
growl. In any tongue.
It's not the note a bell strikes
but the gesture of ringing,
its simple suggestion:
Someone's out there,
attempting in the dark distance
to tell us something,
recognizing our capacity
to hear—even when
we won't listen, even if
we're limited to a language,
one that may be too stingy
to offer a word for bell.

A mother coos. The child
responds in gibberish,
the wordless nonsense
our connective tissue,
as binding as laughter,
more nuanced than blood.

Masculinity

I learned its meaning from my mother.

Warm   like the compress
                I steadied
                against her stoma.

Gentle   exertion
                as I attached
                her colostomy bag.

Reassuring   eye contact
                when she apologized
                "for this god-awful mess."

Ready   to remind her:
                the countless times
                she changed me
                as a child.

Grateful   to mine affection
                wherever
                it might be found.

I've Been Told My Birth Mother Believed in Aliens

That when she was dying of breast cancer,
she blamed her pain on things that had fallen
from the sky. She was not angry at those things,
I've been told. She was not scared of the aliens.

I wonder if she was scared of us. The six children
she birthed and abandoned or surrendered.
If maybe we seemed more alien than extraterrestrials,
more painful than her cancer, than the anger

she might have assumed we harbored toward her.
I've been told she ran off to Florida in the 50s.
And I wonder if Florida sounded more glamourous
to a small-town Pennsylvania girl back then.

I've been told she lived for a time in Hollywood,
Florida. And I wonder if she loved sending relatives
postcards from there, if she pined for the Hollywood
in California. She left her husband, I've been told,

in the 60s, leaving my older brothers with him.
And I wonder what made her leave. And wonder
why that impresses me more than it saddens me.
Imagining a rebel woman escaping a prescribed fate,

not some villain. No, I've been told she was girlish,
sweet. And I wonder if maybe she was just scared,
if maybe she was angry and scared of her anger.
I wonder if she felt more at home with us

as aliens, out there somewhere, faraway. And
wonder if she wondered about us, wondering
if we were angry or scared, or if we wondered
about her, waiting for her to make contact.

In Tamika's Basement

Sorta stoned from the spray paint fumes.

 * *TWISTED FUCKEN SISTER* *

Alternating black and hot-pink letters
scrawled across the white cotton sheet
lifted from her mother's linen closet.

We're not gonna take it, Tamika sang,
rattling both paint cans like maracas.
*If I can't hang it from the balcony,
I'll wear it as a cape. Rush the stage!*

My 14-year-old Superwoman. Unafraid:
ID-checking bouncers, mosh-pit metalheads,
her mother. *What're you gonna tell her?*

I'm sleeping over your house—duh!

An all-access pass. To my bedroom.
The demure boy. (A *twisted* sister?)
As her accomplice I bubbled
like the second coat of hot pink.

Shivering in shorts, she kissed me *G'night*
beneath the corner streetlight, my shadow
spilling into hers—our odd shape a tattoo
on the asphalt we would one day leave.

Dog Days

Already exhausted after a morning conference
with that team of butterflies who dart from topic
to topic—interesting yes, but ever evasive—
she'll conduct a thorough inspection of the Koi pond,
reminding that territorial frog he's merely a temp here.
After all, he doesn't have the expertise to help
thin out that host of sparrows cluttering her in-box.
She'd consider paging the Pugs next door
for back up, but they're lazy and lack authority.
So she'll just do it herself, patrolling the perimeters
of this yard—her corner office—hardly flinching
when someone calls her a bitch. No matter how
shabby or chic, this is *her* castle. And she's always
on call, multi-tasking even on coffee breaks when
lounging in a white patch of noon sun, she prevents
her boss's favorite Persian rug from bleaching.
Never expecting a Christmas bonus or pat on the back—
a bowl of fresh water and occasional table scrap
her modest wage for a job well done.

Mother Medusa

They forget you were a sister, a daughter,
and a mother. Yeah, so easy for them
to picture the severing of your head—
some great heroic feat for some great hero
with a name that escapes them as easily
as his cause to kill you—he owed the king
a wedding gift! That's right. No registering
at Tiffany's back then. Just bring the couple
a serpent-haired head. A statement piece
for the mantel. But would anyone point out
over casual pre-gladiator-game libations
just how you came to be coiffed so?
Athena's punishment for a gorgon girl
who had the nerve to get raped by Poseidon
in the goddess's own temple. Maybe
that's a form of divine slut-shaming
mere mortals couldn't possibly grasp.
But there's no name for what came next:
Athena donning your head on her shield.
Medusa, they forget and still forget how
you gave birth from your gaping neck:
a white-winged horse. Pegasus, a name
more known than the great what's-his-face
hero, who co-opted a mother's power
to make mortal flesh into lasting stone.
Atlas—no match for you—now an epic hunk
of rocky mountain range in North Africa.
Yes, you changed the face of this earth
with your face. Oh, great maker of statues—
fierce mother whose glare could freeze
any child in his tracks—when you died,
did you see how your offspring flew?

"That's Ms. Pride to You"

As thin as you are, almost papery—
a ragged flag wisping about in the breeze
created by the current of floats and marchers—
I spotted you waving stiffly yet regally:
Hostess to a nearly empty bus.

Like a fragile branch in a dense forest
of muscular trunks and glittery foliage—
your saggy arms and mottled hands
inspire some boys behind the barricades
to make an extra trip to the gym this week,
spread the sunscreen on a little thicker.

Give it up, honey! There's a run in those hose—
No, wait! WAIT! It's just a run in his skin.

Beaming, you show a little more leg.
Like an old aunt grateful to have family
at the holidays, you hear only youth
in the cruelty. You straighten your sash.
Boys will be boys, you might proclaim
if there were another Stonewaller beside you,
if they hadn't all died. Better yet—
Boys will be girls.

Not even the ghost of a beauty queen
veiled by time or your five o'clock shadow,
as you sweat, beaded like your brocade pumps
in this late June heat on this packed Village street—
the back of your satin gown speckled like
a worker's flannel—I see a teacher on that bus,
a lesson for all in your lifted skirt.

My Sister Michele Never Read the Book

        or traveled internationally herself,
but when she dropped her daughter Kimberly
at airport security for her first trip abroad
(ten days in Israel), Michele took her hands,
stared into her eyes, and said, "Remember, hon:
*Eat. Pray. Love...*or just get a little action.
What—calm down! You're 21! Now go,
get to your gate before I start blubbering."

In Her Voice

"There's the sound of birds rising…"
—Stevie Nicks

Not descending. Rising.
As if punctuating clouds,
all commas.

Or the stifled whimper
of a mother wolf
seeing her runt go limp.
Composure for the survivors' sake.

Maybe some lover's hand
lifting, yoga like,
finger outstretched like those
it points to: Michelangelo's ceiling.

A sultry glance
from behind oversized sunglasses
saying without saying,
I dig your hip-huggers.

That umbrella fringe trembling,
pre-storm—sand spray softly
prickling newly browned legs.

Or that woman adjusting her sari
in the hot dry breeze,
always a few steps ahead
of her husband.

And girls, definitely girls—*la la*-ing,
twirling before dusty mirrors,
where they spy more beautiful
versions of themselves.

Carpetbagger

Back when you could smoke on a plane
my parents asked if I could manage
to sit by myself in Non-smoking. "Just ten
rows behind us," my mother pleaded,
"next to this nice lady here," who nodded,
as if they'd previously struck the deal—
our tickets awkwardly split (3 Smoking/
1 Non) and my twin sister refusing to budge.
"Oh!" chirped the lady. "We'll have fun!"
Like some Mary Poppins catching a lift
while her umbrella was in the shop?
The floppy carpet bag like a pillow
or old dog in her lap, the thick tapestry
of rich greens and purples deeper than
her pastel outfit and orange lipstick.
She waited for my mother to shuffle
back to the cloudy side of the plane.
"So you like games?" she asked. "I bet
you don't hate candy either, huh—
didn't think so. Visiting my grandsons
in Tampa. Luckily this bag's bottomless!"
She patted it, as if it really were a dog.
I thought I saw it breathing and asked
for a peek but she put a finger to her lips
as the safety instructions began—
the scariest part: When they showed
(with cheerful smiles) air masks popping
from the ceiling. I pictured my father
with one strapped to his stubbly face,
cigarette still in hand as we braced
for a crash landing. Then tried to focus
instead on my new friend: Her hands,

veiny, folded on the leather-lipped mouth
of that magical bag. In three hours' time
it spat *Star Wars* cards, a Chinese finger trap,
crayons (new ones!) and a Scooby Doo
coloring book, Milk Duds, Blow Pops...
My jaw too exhausted from a Tootsie Roll
to accept the stick of Juicy Fruit. "To help
keep your ears from clogging!" she said.
But I was fine, I told her as we descended.
I could manage. I was completely clear.

Sonnet for the Dowager Countess

Lines from *Downton Abbey*

Why Does Every Day Involve a Fight with an American?

Please don't speak that man's name, we are about to eat.

He was too like his mother and a nastier woman never drew breath.

I don't dislike him. I just don't like him. Which is quite different.

So what? I have plenty of friends I don't like.

Why do you always have to pretend to be nicer than the rest of us?

He's a fortune hunter...a pleasant one I admit, but a fortune hunter.

He's political and a writer. I can make something out of that.

We can't have him assassinated...I suppose.

No doubt you will regard this as rather unorthodox.

We must work with what we've got to minimize the scandal.

One can't go to pieces at the death of every foreigner.

I dare say I'm beyond impropriety.

This sort of thing is all very well in novels.

But then I'm old. Things may be different now.

Cherry Grove Carla

could be Charo's Italian cousin
with that bleached blonde ponytail
and her *coochy-coochy-coo*-ing
any neighbor's roaming pooch poo-ing
on her pink flamingo-dotted lawn.
But it's free fertilizer, honey, she reminds
her frowning butch girlfriend,
a spicy fit 50 known for swearing
at Tea that she was cradle-robbed
by her *(Yes, 70-something Cougar!)* Carla
who on chilly days still sports
frayed denim short shorts tight enough
to make even the Speedo-ed
Pines boys blush when they stop by
for a quick *Hi* or drop in to sing *Girl,*
where ya been, dragging a new roommate
from their summer share, too skeptical
to believe she really—*No! Really?*—
still wears those signature yellow
leg warmers with chunky platforms
and micro-bikini, clunking along
the boardwalk, humming classic Disco
to the demure deer who trail her,
their sunburned Snow White brimming
with years of her own *fairytales*
she might've been tempted to sell
had her mother not insisted
noble women who know how to kiss right
are too busy living life to tell.

My Niece Kimberly

                    was in her highchair
when at 23 I shut off the kitchen tv
and stammered, "I'm gay,"
expecting my quiet father to slip
into an even deeper unblinking silence
or sobs from my mother,
mourning her framed mental photos—
white silken chuppahs and handsome grandkids
named Montlack—fragmenting not like
the ceremonial glass under heel
but like the uncleared dinner plates
I'd imagined she'd throw (but didn't)
while Kimberly would continue
to nudge soggy pale peas
across a scratch-proof surface
unconcerned as one by one
they approached and fell
over the beveled safety edge
designed to contain
what parents expected
a child to eat.

Alice (in Lawn-guy-land)

ducked out of our parents' BBQs, into the house.
For some friggen air, she'd groan, lighting a cigarette.
I mean, the heat's o-pressive out there. O! Pressive!
Leaning in to whisper, *Uchh, and such old fogies.*
Alice was 53. The other parents 60. *I'll just hang
with you kids. Listen to The Bon Jovies and whatnot.*

Then she'd eyeball my sister. *Now, listen here—
whateva you can't tell your motha, come tell me.
Ok? I never had daughters…* My sister promised.
Even when Alice said, *Abortions, birth control pills,
bail for a boyfriend. Whateva!* My sister was 13.

We never told Alice much—afraid she'd snitch—
but still loved her. Thick, oversized glasses,
Alice engraved across the bottom of the left lens.
Rayon rhinestone-studded sweat suits ruffling
as she sashayed through rooms. Thinning Jewfro.
Like Richard Simmons—we loved him too.
But knew never to draw comparisons.

I held back our setters whenever she visited,
my mother demanding I keep them from leaping.
They loved Alice too. Entering cautiously,
manicured hands extended. *The dawgs!* she'd cry.
The dawgs! Then glare at me. *I'm diabetic!*

Took me months to figure out the Diabetes Walk
wasn't to cure dog phobias. *Oh, for god sakes!*
my mother laughed. *She's afraid of being scratched.
Not healing properly.* Sore, I almost mentioned
the abortion offers. But knew Alice was on our side—
she **did** trust me to save her from the dogs. Plus,

occasionally she'd slip my sister a drag or two.
Saying she never could enjoy a smoke by herself.

Mother,

I could write about
your greeting whenever I came home:
Hungry? Lemme open a can of tuna...

Or how you adopted three kids (and how
we—well loved—never considered peeking
at our files). Maybe a few light lines

about how you blushed with pride
when a bowling teammate announced,
Ya hit the queer trifecta, Claire!
—a lesbian daughter, gay son and
my drag-queenish twin (Sorry, Sis,
must be all those animal prints...).

You—Dad's Lions Club Lioness—
hosting seasonal Dances for the Blind,
getting dolled up, fussing, spritzing,
as he yelled, *Come on already, Claire!*
Who in da hell's gonna see you there?

I could mention your humongous handbags,
surprisingly light, brimming with crumpled
tissues, keys, Trident gum and eyeshadow:
that 60s seafoam green you believed
complimented crimson hair. How

as you aged you grew fascinated by
the weather, calling me daily in the city
to discuss the heat or humidity. Until I forbade
the topic. Unless it was catastrophic. Saying,
Okay, okay—this is your big day, Mom!
when you were hospitalized hours before
Hurricane Irene, propped up and IV-ed,

penciling in your menu for the week
(*Yay! Tuesday's salmon with carrot puree!*)
while binge-watching your favorite
meteorologist on NBC.

How you'd respond to our snarky teenage
jabs (or some road hog) with a *Chuck you!*
Or a *Friggen idiot!* and still pause to excuse
your "French."

Mother, I could write a poem about any
or all these things. But what I really want
to write is this plain artless plea: *I miss you,
Mom. And miss being someone's son.* So
open up a can! Tell me the forecast again.
How tomorrow looks like it might be clear.
Or just less cloudy.

Stevie

What else can be said about the aftertaste of her alto?
A 170-proof vodka upstaged by its wispy twist of tangerine peel.
Classical ballet performed in chunky platform boots on the cusp
of an unclimbable cliff. The chalk cliffs of Dover, say, something
nearly sheer, practically pure. A crystalline snow drift at dawn
pockmarked with paw prints left by an unleashed Labrador.
See how her disciples swerve to that lush vibrato—hungry
Hansels and Gretels leaping into the mouth of her oven.

Ruth

1935—Amelia Earhart was the first
to fly solo from Honolulu to California.
The Dust Bowl rolled out record heat.
Where at 16 could you have flown or blown?

Surely not far from the family that took in
your baby girl. Like your biblical namesake:
Where you go I will go...Even buried
in the hometown that called you *hussy*.

No aprons or arthritis in my imaginary
portrait of you. Just a faceless silhouette.
A marble cameo laced tight as a noose
around the neck of a voiceless woman.

Ruth—Grandmother—you are a stitch
in the lining of an inside pocket, a vintage
jacket I have never worn. Hanging
in a dark locked wardrobe that smells
just like me.

Father

---

*"My father had dignity. At the
end of his life his life began
to wake in me."*

—Sharon Olds

One Sparrow

circles the bridge,
as if to signify a need, its arcs
nearly complete, dismantled
figure 8s.

The river wrinkles
its reflection: like a shooting
black star aimed for its place
in an unfinished constellation.

Where is the flock?

Sky on the cusp of twilight,
the sparrow sweeps in the dark,
and your voice dangles from it,
my ears recognizing this much:

Son…

You were a man of few words
in life too.

And then there was fire…

Fourth of Julys, we'd collect in the court
for volleyball or SPUD, waiting for dark,
when the more daring dads emerged
from BBQ pits with fireworks scored on trips
to Miami or Myrtle Beach. Though the most
daring hadn't shelled out a week's pay
on Roman Candles and Chinese Spinners.
The creative (or *cheap)* ones could make light
and thunder with household items, plain junk.

Mr. Machete—armed with a grip of steel wool
and a twine lasso—decorated the air with a swarm
of orange 'fireflies' whirling out in spirals
that made smaller kids take refuge behind larger.
How legendary he'd become when a spark landed
in Mr. Butchen's shirt pocket, proudly stuffed
with half a dozen bottle rockets—the pocket
his daughter would describe as *charred*
after he returned from the ER, breast bandaged.
(Was that why they were called SOS pads?)

Even my own father got into the act—my dad
who, when we were lucky, splurged on a pack
of candy store firecrackers, the wimpy stuff
Mr. Softee sold off his truck to minors. Not worth
a second look if it couldn't blow off a few fingers,
at least momentarily render us deaf. But my father
spiced it up, dropping a 'cracker into an empty Bud can.

Then the strange pride burning like a fuse up my spine
as everyone watched, waiting to see if the can
would splinter. My father—himself stepping back
(with us) into the line of lounge chairs and coolers—
could have been a spy, a fugitive, an astronaut

strapping himself in. No longer the overworked,
overweight husband/father/mechanic recovering
from a second heart attack, second mortgage.
For in those sizzling seconds he was King
of his court, while I and the other kids—
from a respectful distance—paid homage
to this middle-aged, ordinary man
who, for a brief but dazzling moment,
was a provider of light, creator of fire.

My Father's Workshop

The familiar inferno:
my boy-self sweltering
away half his summer
in a basement boiler room,
my father pointing
his pocket flashlight
at a television's tubes
or a drill's stubborn bit,
always investigating
like a makeshift cop
patrolling the beat of things
and *how* they worked
while I was distracted by
why—this miniature hammer
too small for his fleshy grip
or that garden shovel
when we had no garden.

I was taught to strip and stain
shelves, chairs, tabletops,
told to *Do things right*
or not do them at all—
my father offering himself:
a rough whetstone on which
to sharpen myself into a man
like him, one who knew *how*
to repair what already was
while I schemed ways to swap
my sweaty skin calloused
by his raw-material realms
for a lecture hall, a library—
some well-lit, sawdust-less place
where a flashlight wouldn't help
see what was happening.

Early October

House cats scramble as if they know
something to kill lurks in the growing dark
beyond the lace curtains, a chill
rising like the bristles of their tails.

The neighbor boy jabs a grimy ratchet
into the open hood of his '65 Camaro,
shimmying spark plugs until they slip,
smacking the concrete garage floor.

When did he stop trick-or-treating?
Trading gumdrops and Good & Plenty
for greasy forearms and lacquered girls.
He kicks at leaves stuck to a wet tire.

Soon mothers will holler through screen doors,
stern ten-minute warnings. It won't matter.
Hungry or not, the kids will dare to linger
on browning lawns, certain there's still time.

When you say *Uncle*

I sometimes hear *Father.*

A foreign country
I never planned to visit.

Still you take me there
when you say *Uncle.*
Feeding me a half-eaten cookie.
Repeatedly asking your mother
why I have to go home.

When you say *Uncle,*
I realize I am home.

When you say *Uncle,*
it is enough.

Family Affair

My sister Michele called me from the car:
We just got the puppy! A Beagle! Adorable!
In the background a frenzy of traffic, giggles,
barking. *We phoned so you'd be here with us,*
my mother yelled. *Come see him, Uncle Mike!*
my niece squealed. Sure, I said. This weekend!

Dad wants you to name him now, Michele said.
Name him? How? I hadn't even seen the dog.

I know, she said. *But you're the writer—so*
he thinks you should name him. And I agree.
Mom wants Clint. After Eastwood. But I was like
hell no! I can just see her in the yard calling him.
So? I said. *So?* she whispered. *It sounds like **clit***
when she says it—what'll the neighbors think?

Understood. My mother called my friend Jennifer:
Jenavah. My ex Jamal: Ja-mawl. (And dogs: dawgs.)

And let's give him a gay name! my father blurted.

A gay name? Was he joking or overly medicated—
this puppy meant to cheer him after his last stroke.
Why a gay name? I asked.

I dunno, he said. *I just want a gay name.*
And my gay son to name him.

Well, what's a gay name?

You tell me, he said. *You're the expert.*

Oscar Wilde? I offered.

Who da hell is that?

How about Harvey Milk then?

Harvey WHAT?

Finally I asked my mother to choose, reminding her
to say it was my idea. *Okay, we'll call him Beau,*
she said. *That way he can be anyone's sweetheart.*

Esmeralda

As real as Santa or the Easter Bunny
whenever my mother muttered your name.
Your father's late for dinner again!
Bet he's with his girlfriend Esmeralda.

You sounded so exotic. Like Mexican cities
where *The Price Is Right* sent hysterical winners.
Foreign. Sexy. Naughty. I could picture you:
long wavy brown hair, a red strapless dress,
sleek as one of my mother's Virginia Slims.

She tossed salad in her Tupperware,
letting the dog eat whatever greens fell
to the linoleum. My sister offering to call
the station again—as if she wanted to
catch him. Not see if our mother was lying.

Did you ever meet Esmeralda? I asked.
What's she like? It never dawned on me
to wonder if my mother was jealous.
To ask why she was so casual about it.
It never dawned on me to be afraid
my parents might divorce, that this *had*
to be a joke, that my pot-bellied father—
same oily work pants daily (pale, hairy
butt crack peeking out despite the belt)—
couldn't possibly have a mistress.

When he trudged in, my sister and I checked
his collarless t-shirt for lipstick. Perfume
strong enough to out-stink the gasoline.
A long silky brown strand stuck somewhere
to his grime-streaked brow. Always nothing.

Dinner's cold, Howie, my mother growled.
Maybe you already dined...with Esmeralda!

Rubbing his belly, he chuckled. *I sure did!*
But you know I always have room for seconds.

Back in the Workshop

We could have been Alchemists
conjuring beneath the naked bulb
as bald as my father's head
sweating in the boiler's heat.
Summoned from cartoons to steady
a board for sanding and staining
or a dining room table leg
too fine for the vice's toothy grip,
I was his sole accomplice. A boy
teased for having an airy imagination
and tripping over my long legs.
Holed-off in a stale basement corner,
charting my mother's steps in the kitchen above,
we were hushed Alcatraz inmates
ready to dig. I knew about the phone tap
hooked casually on the rack, camouflaged
by the other wires and tools. On loan
from a neighbor (a phone company retiree)
to monitor my older sister's calls.
At 7, I knew it was the only way
to keep her from running away,
so sure it would never be used on me.
Why—sleeves rolled like his,
wasn't I part of the solution,
an extension of his own hands?

Legend

That story about your father as a teen
some uncle or cousin digs up and dusts off
at a diner after a funeral or in a hospital
waiting room. How the skinny, mild-mannered
mama's boy stood up that frigid night
to your frigid, no-nonsense granddad,
over some insignificant something or other,
refusing to back down in the back seat
even when threatened on the Verrazano:
*I'll stop this car right here and you'll walk
back to the Bronx!* Your father, unflinching,
cowboy quiet, incapable of cowering,
maybe to impress his mother, shotgun
stoic: *Just leave the boy alone, already.*
Yeah, your father, demanding they stop,
halfway over that bridge, an hour after dusk,
halting traffic, deaf to horns, blind to
middle fingers, gently closing his door,
so as not to startle his mother, gently
opening the screen door miles later
when he arrived home an hour before
dawn, so as not to startle his mother,
who would wake that crisp morning
to her boy, once seen and seldom heard,
suddenly turned man of his word.

Parade

My father built a cage for me:
two-by-fours jerry-rigged
to a neighbor's rusty flatbed,
my sister trimming it with streamers—
blue and gold, Lions Club colors.

Reminded by my father's friends
to stand tall in my red velvet vest
and top hat, I gripped the leather
whip *Like you mean it,* my uncle said,
muffled beneath his furry lion head.

The streamers wilting in the heat
as we rocked past sunburned spectators
lining the curb, my free hand
clenching a splintery bar. *Give 'em
a show,* my uncle growled, pawing
at his mane. *Like you mean it!*

I didn't like being reminded. I didn't
like the crowd as it swelled: *Whip him,
wuss! What're you afraid of?* I knew

my sister would say she could have
done a better job. And she would have.
My father's eyes in the rear-view.
I tried to strike, to thrash—the lash
as ill-fitting as my costume. I let

the whip fall to the truck's bed,

turning my back on the crowd, my uncle,
my father's mirror. A surge of blood
into my palms as if my life-lines
were being carved right there
by the same tame power of resistance
spilling through the bars so hard,
the streamers finally lifted.

Granddaddy Jess

Four years old, I balanced
on that bar top—my first stage—
speckled with the shine of new quarters
the regulars tossed at my feet.
Some day it'd be roses and baby's breath
cushioning the path of my platforms
(six- or eight-inch heels) elevating me
as Granddaddy's hands had
lifting me up to that bar.
My Granddaddy,
a country-western singer
who never really made it
beyond the saloon circuit
of smaller Southwestern cities,
always said or sang or scolded,
"Sing like you mean it, Stevie!
Like you mean it."

Today sequins, rhinestones, silvery threads
in brocaded chiffons shipped from India.
And the sweat-and-tear gloss
that could come only from a song
sung with meaning, sung with urgency,
to please a disappointed Granddaddy
so he might see beyond his failures
to the child still bowing there
in a glittering shower of coins.

From Poland with Love

Now that he's long gone
and I'm old enough to care—
to even think to ask—
what it was like to board
a ship as a teen, by himself,
leaving behind a string
of sisters, his weary parents
and an even wearier country—
      I'm left to imagine
those hazy scenes (in sepia)
my parents tried to recall
as they sensed it was nearly time
they too left this world, where
he—the lanky boy who would
become my sturdy grandfather—
once stood huffing at a turnstile,
supposedly coinless but suave enough
to charm a nickel and a smile
out of that cool Russian girl,
promising an ice cream cone
to settle the score. Chocolate?
Vanilla? Nah. Must've been
a livelier flavor (by turn-of-the-century
standards), considering he chewed
Fruit Stripe gum into his eighties,
always a pack in the pocket
of his trousers, ironed daily
even after his cool Russian's ride
ended somewhere in the 70s
and she grew cooler
in the New Jersey cemetery
where he'd bought a plot
for ten, somehow knowing
before they had even met—
he'd have a family to rest beside,
it making perfect sense to reserve
his place, having gone
to all that trouble to get here.

End Game

Mornings before work my sister Michele,
in her dingy oversized T-shirt nightie
(*Still In My 20s And YOU'RE Not!*)
itself nearing twenty, wheeled my father
out to the patio for coffee and a cigarette—
"He's smoked this long," she'd tell our mother.
"It might be what's keeping him alive.")—
ready for another round of ghost hunting,
my father swearing some days that his own
parents were sitting on the garden bench,
their backs to him, gray heads bent downward.
The first time he pointed it out, we panicked,
sure it was one more sign of his departure,
and begged doctors to tell us it was the dosage,
which could be adjusted to bring him back
to our dimension. Sometimes he'd reach
from the recliner for his Dalmatian, dead
ten years, then reach for me with eyes
that wordlessly requested an explanation,
always unalarmed by my saying nothing
was there. "To hell there's not," he'd say,
chuckling the way he did when I told him
I was a vegetarian (*Oh, so White Castles
don't count?*). "Don't you see?" he asked
Michele, poised for his dare. "Right there!
They're plain as day." She slipped off her
furry slippers to tiptoe across the muddy lawn,
calling, "Here? **Here**? How about here, Daddy?"
As he'd gently steer her: "Yup, that's it…
another step forward. You see them now?"
Her Jackie O sunglasses held back her bangs
as if they were what had been blocking her sight.
"Grandma?" she whispered. "You **sure**, Daddy?"
"Yeah!" he hollered. "You're standing on them!"
"Oh my God!" she gasped, jumping back
an easy foot or two. "Daddy, don't—don't!
They'll think I'm rude."

Finding My Biological Parents

Could confirm ethnicity.
Surrender my mystery.
Glean medical history.
Predict genetic catastrophe.

Kiss Me, I'm Italian!
Kiss Me, I'm Puerto Rican!
Kiss Me, I'm Jewish!

When I was a boy there were no T-shirts
that said *Kiss Me, I'm Adopted!*
or *Kiss Me, Your Guess Is As Good As Mine!*

I was kissed plenty though.
By a mother and father
who required no reason
or fuzzy iron-on letters
instructing them to do so.

They knew their medical histories
and still died deaths similar
to those of their parents—
how's that for family tradition?

My DNA may not be a map
of their ancestral neighborhoods
or even in the same hemisphere.

But what I don't know
will kill me just as dead
as they are. And I will rot
into the earth as easily
or reluctantly as they did.

Leaving the Body

Will it resemble a waterlogged child
refusing to abandon the frigid pool?
Too short-sighted to anticipate the sun-
warmed towel, an end to shivering.

Or will it be more of a remembering
than a forgetting? Like entering the hallway
to a first bedroom. The kind of familiarity
no photograph or scent could foster.

Maybe a dismissal. Of awkwardness:
a worn crutch no longer needed,
high heels kicked off after work.

Or maybe a sigh, spirits hammocked,
as our craggy shells wash ashore—
meat slurped by a celestial mouth,
its bite benign as a kiss.

Do Our Parents Ever Really Die?

Or are they just on vacation.
Maybe they never budged
from your childhood home.
Cozy on the couch, waiting
for their favorite "program."
Your mother's definitely there
in the way you slice open
an avocado before it's ripe,
or how you treat yourself
to a hot fudge sundae
just because it's raining.
Can't you feel your shoulders
hunch like hers, as if to say
Yeah, I'm being naughty. SO?
And isn't your father poking
fun again when you discover
his belly has become your own.
Sometimes I can smell them
when I hold Beau, their orphan
Beagle. His eyes guilty, as if
he's stolen their socks again.
As if he knows he smells
like tuna salad and cigarettes.
Like the 60's luncheonette
where my mother served
milk shakes and egg creams.
Sometimes I'm certain
that's where she's gone.
The place where she learned
to stack the perfect BLT
for the man who would be
my father. He's still around
for sure. I hear him groan
every time I open the freezer
to find some pig must've eaten
the last ice cream sandwich,
only to realize that yeah, okay,
okay, it was probably me.

Unceremonial

Leave my body untended.
Consider it less a wreck,
more a ruin, a slow recline
into the landscape, soft clay
ready for the cosmic kiln.

Just let my molecules be
inhaled by the planet, exhaled
during its next little sneeze,
my unremarkable particles,
tiny satellites dusting
the atmosphere.

Spare the niceties: Don't
bloat my casings with plastic,
over groom my beard, stuff me
into a designer suit finer
than anything I ever wore.

It's all packaging. Sugary
glaze on a stale donut. Like
selecting the perfect outfit
to wear to an orgy—no,
simply deliver me
the way I came in.

Thank You

To my family and friends.

To Julia Markus, for believing in me.

Raymond Hammond, for believing in my work.

Richard Blanco, Rachel Eliza Griffiths, Joseph Millar, and David Trinidad, for your generous blurbs.

And Alessandro Brusa, for translating my poems into Italian for the Bologna in Lettere 2020 Festival.

To my writer friends and friends who support my writing: Will Baker, Amanda Bradley, Kerry Carnahan, Jon Carter, Cyrus Cassells, Peter Covino, Blas Falconer, Stephanie Fairyington, Ellen First, Francesco Gagliardi, David Groff, Scott Hightower, Bradley Nelson, Marilyn Nelson, Trent Pollard, and Soraya Shalforoosh.

VCCA and Ragdale Foundation, for their writer residencies.

Terrence O'Sullivan and Gary Vena, for being such gentlemen.

Christopher Shields, for beautiful cover art.

Marc Brudzinski, for the back cover seahorse.

Dorianne Laux, for the author photo.

Special thanks to DoJo (Dorianne and Joe) for inviting me to write with them, showing me how to welcome the muses more frequently.

And boundless thanks to the muses.

Lightning Source UK Ltd.
Milton Keynes UK
UKHW011530110221
378627UK00003B/920